Everything You Need to Know About *Hepatitis C*

Hepatitis C is a serious disease that affects more than 170 million people around the world.

Everything You Need to Know About *Hepatitis C*

Chris Hayhurst

The Rosen Publishing Group, Inc.
New York

Published in 2003 by The Rosen Publishing Group, Inc.
29 East 21st Street, New York, NY 10010

Copyright © 2003 by The Rosen Publishing Group, Inc.

First Edition

All rights reserved. No part of this book may be reproduced in any form without permission in writing from the publisher, except by a reviewer.

Library of Congress Cataloging-in-Publication Data

Hayhurst, Chris.
Everything you need to know about Hepatitis C / by Chris Hayhurst.—1st ed.
p. cm. — (The need to know library)
Includes bibliographical references and index.
ISBN 978-1-4358-8889-0
1. Hepatitis C—Juvenile literature. [1. Hepatitis C. 2. Diseases.]
I. Title. II. Series.
RC848.H425 H39 2002
616.3'623—dc21

2001006633

Manufactured in the United States of America

Contents

	Introduction	6
Chapter 1	What Is Hepatitis C?	9
Chapter 2	Contracting the Hepatitis C Virus	16
Chapter 3	Getting Tested for Hepatitis C	29
Chapter 4	Living with Hepatitis C	37
Chapter 5	The Future of Hepatitis C	45
	Glossary	55
	Where to Go for Help	57
	For Further Reading	61
	Bibliography	62
	Index	63

Introduction

There's a good chance that up until now you've never heard of hepatitis C. This is because hepatitis C, unlike AIDS or other more famous diseases, is hardly noticeable in most of its victims. When the disease is contracted, the infected person doesn't become sick right away. In fact, if the person is lucky, he or she may never become ill at all. Diseases such as this receive very little attention from the public. After all, what's the point of worrying about a disease if it's not serious?

This is a computer illustration of the hepatitis C virus, a virus more common than HIV.

The problem is that hepatitis C is serious. The disease affects more than 170 million people around the world. In the United States alone, at least 4 million people have hepatitis C. More people have hepatitis C than HIV, the virus that causes AIDS. Most of these people will never develop dangerous health problems from the disease, but those who do can die.

Some health professionals have called hepatitis C the "silent epidemic." It's silent, they say, because the disease tends to progress slowly, taking a long time to cause serious health problems. It's an epidemic because of the huge number of people who are infected.

Hepatitis C

In this book you'll learn all about hepatitis C—what it is, how it affects the human body, how it's spread, and what you can do to keep from getting infected. You'll also learn how doctors test for hepatitis C, how they go about treating it, and what it's like to live with the disease. Finally, you'll catch a glimpse of the future and the promise that new anti–hepatitis C medications and technologies—some already in use, some still in development—hold for the world. It will be a long time before hepatitis C is no longer a threat to human health. Until then, all you can do is learn how to protect yourself.

Chapter 1
What Is Hepatitis C?

There are five different strains of the hepatitis virus. Doctors refer to the different variations by letter—A, B, C, D, and E. Hepatitis A is a relatively minor disease. It's transmitted, or passed, from one person to another mainly through food and water contaminated with infected feces, and it is referred to as "infectious hepatitis." Hepatitis A hardly ever requires medical treatment. Hepatitis B is another type of hepatitis. It's transmitted through blood and through the sharing of body fluids, usually during sexual intercourse, and can be fatal. Vaccines are available for both hepatitis A and hepatitis B. The vaccines provide protection against the diseases for many years.

Hepatitis C

Before the late 1980s, hepatitis A and hepatitis B were the only forms of hepatitis that scientists fully understood. Still, scientists were keenly aware of a third kind of hepatitis—one that was passed from one person to the next through blood transfusions, a process during which blood from one person is donated to another person. For lack of a better name, scientists referred to this other hepatitis as "non-A, non-B hepatitis." All they knew was that it wasn't hepatitis A and it wasn't hepatitis B.

Hepatitis C Facts: Important Facts from the Hepatitis Foundation International

- **Three percent of the world's population is infected with the hepatitis C virus.**
- **Eight countries (Bolivia, Burundi, Cameroon, Egypt, Guinea, Mongolia, Rwanda, and Tanzania) have infection rates of at least 10 percent.**
- **Ninety percent of hepatitis C sufferers throughout the world cannot afford the cost of treatment.**

What Is Hepatitis C?

But then, in 1989, molecular biologists made a new discovery. As they closely analyzed the blood cells of a patient with non-A, non-B hepatitis, they saw something in the cells they had never seen before. There, in a part of the cell known as RNA, was the virus that caused this strange disease. The scientists turned to the alphabet for guidance. They named the virus hepatitis C.

Hepatitis C's Effect on the Body

The hepatitis C virus, or HCV, is the virus that is responsible for causing hepatitis C. Other illnesses are caused by other viruses. AIDS, for example, is caused by HIV, the human immunodeficiency virus. Influenza, better known as the flu, is caused by an entirely different virus.

Viruses can be passed from one person to the next. HCV, which so far has only been found in humans and chimpanzees, is a blood-borne virus. It's spread mainly through blood-to-blood contact between an infected individual and another person.

Many people who contract hepatitis C never notice any symptoms. They can go for years without even knowing they have the disease. They live their lives, for the most part, just like everyone else.

Hepatitis C

But some people aren't so lucky. The real danger of hepatitis C is the damage it's capable of doing to the liver. Liver damage can occur in patients who have had hepatitis C for a very long time. When you've had a disease for a long period of time—for months or years—the illness is referred to as "chronic." Most people with hepatitis C develop a chronic form of the disease. In other words, once you get hepatitis C it tends to stick around.

The word "hepatitis" comes from *hepa*, the Latin word for liver, and *itis*, a suffix that means "inflammation." Quite literally, hepatitis is a disease of the liver. The hepatitis virus attacks and damages liver cells. As a result, the liver becomes inflamed, or swollen. If the disease is allowed to progress, it can eventually destroy the liver's ability to work.

You need a healthy liver in order to survive. It is a vital part of the body. It fights infections, stops bleeding, and removes toxins from the bloodstream. As the second largest organ in the body (only the skin, which is also an organ, is bigger), it is responsible for thousands of critical reactions and processes related to the body's overall functioning. The liver is so important, in fact, that it's capable of rebuilding itself by generating new cells to replace damaged ones.

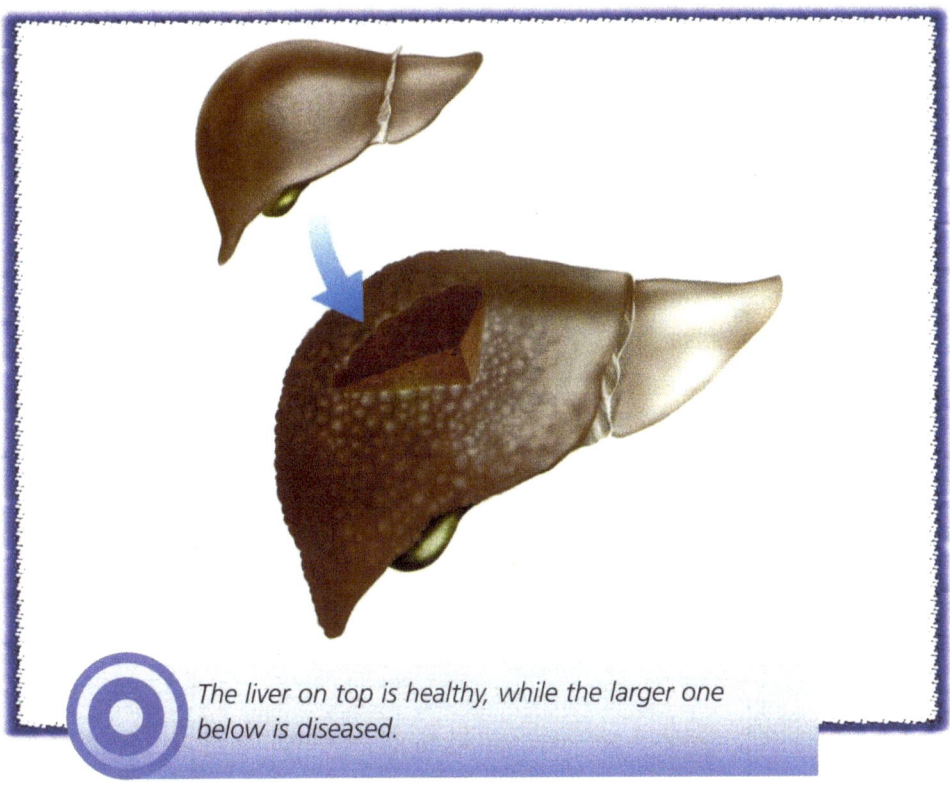

The liver on top is healthy, while the larger one below is diseased.

Unfortunately for those with chronic forms of hepatitis C, sometimes the liver can no longer repair itself. At this point, it begins to lose its ability to function as well as it should. In very serious cases, a condition called cirrhosis sets in. In cirrhosis, dead and damaged liver cells are replaced by tough, fibrous tissue. The liver continues to regenerate, but not back to its usual shape. This abnormal shape and the tissue scarring, called fibrosis, prevent the efficient flow of blood to and through the liver. This, in turn, prevents the liver from doing its job.

Hepatitis C

A Disease Without Borders

Hepatitis C strikes people in countries around the world. The World Health Organization (WHO), which works to prevent and control many different diseases worldwide, estimates that some 170 million people, or 3 percent of the world's population, are infected with the hepatitis C virus. In many parts of the world, hepatitis C is even more of a problem than it is in North America. The 1999 WHO chart below shows just what parts of the world are most affected by hepatitis C.

Region	Total Population (in millions)	Hepatitis C (percentage infected)	Infected Population (in millions)
Africa	602	5.3	31.9
Americas	785	1.7	13.1
Eastern Mediterranean	466	4.6	21.3
Europe	858	1.03	8.9
Southeast Asia	1,500	2.15	32.3
Western Pacific	1,600	3.9	62.2
TOTAL	5,811	3.1	169.7

What Is Hepatitis C?

A Long, Slow Process

Most people progress from acute hepatitis C, a stage of the disease during which few are aware they have it, to chronic hepatitis C. But just because a person has been diagnosed by a doctor as having chronic hepatitis C doesn't mean his or her life will change—at least not overnight. It takes a long time for the cumulative effects of hepatitis C to show up in the liver. In some people, it may be twenty or thirty years between the time they contract the disease and the point where they start to experience major liver damage. Others may die of natural causes that have nothing to do with hepatitis before any symptoms of the disease become apparent. The fact is, dying of chronic liver disease is a long, slow process. And while almost 10,000 people die in the United States each year as a result of complications arising from hepatitis C, millions more survive.

Chapter 2
Contracting the Hepatitis C Virus

Here's the good news: Hepatitis C is hard to get. If you take a few simple precautions, your chances of contracting the disease are slim to none.

Now for the bad news: If you don't take these precautions, you can be at serious risk not only for hepatitis C but also for other life-threatening diseases, such as AIDS.

How Hepatitis C Is Spread

The hepatitis C virus is found primarily in human blood. Because hepatitis C is found in blood, the only way to get the disease is through contact with an infected person's blood. But even then you may get lucky and still not contract the virus. Here's a quick rundown on the ways in which hepatitis C can be spread.

Contracting the Hepatitis C Virus

Intravenous Drug Use

The most common way people contract hepatitis C is through intravenous drug use. According to the Centers for Disease Control and Prevention (CDC), 60 percent of those infected with the virus acquired it by using drugs intravenously. Intravenous drugs are drugs that are injected directly into a vein with a needle. Heroin is one well-known intravenous drug. Users load the heroin into a special syringe that attaches to a needle. They insert the needle under their skin and into a vein, then press down on the syringe to push the drug through the needle and into their bloodstream.

Illegal intravenous drugs like heroin are extremely dangerous even without the threat of disease. People overdose when they take more heroin than their bodies can handle. Overdoses are often fatal. But an equally serious danger with intravenous drugs is the risk that users take when they inject themselves with used needles or syringes. Used needles are contaminated with very small amounts of other people's blood, plus whatever viruses and bacteria are in their blood. When you share a needle or syringe with someone else, you inject his or her blood into your bloodstream along with the drug. If the person you're sharing needles with has hepatitis C, the virus hitches a free ride right into your body.

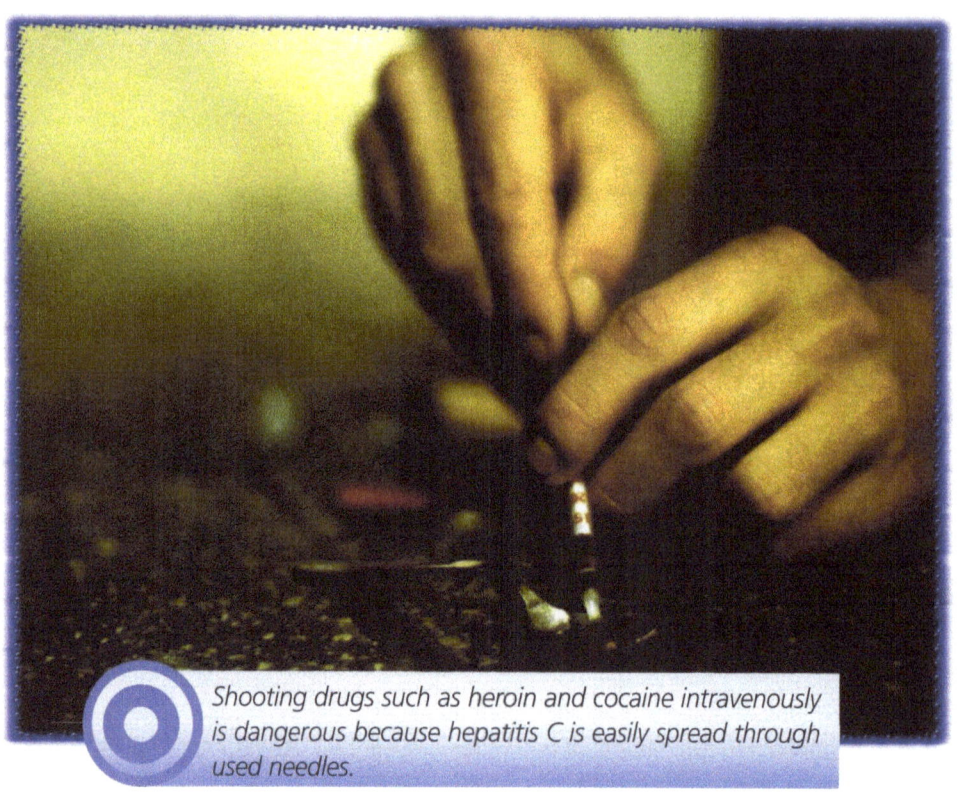

Shooting drugs such as heroin and cocaine intravenously is dangerous because hepatitis C is easily spread through used needles.

Sexual Intercourse

Another way hepatitis C is spread is through sexual intercourse. According to the CDC, 15 percent of people with hepatitis C contracted the virus by having sexual intercourse with an infected person. When two people have unprotected sex, blood from cuts or open sores on one person's body can come in contact with similar cuts or sores on the other person. If a woman has microscopic tears inside her vagina, for example, it's possible that a small amount of blood from a man's penis could enter her bloodstream. Genital tissue is more vulnerable to tears than skin, and such injuries often are so small they are not visible to the eye.

Contracting the Hepatitis C Virus

Unsafe Injections

It's easy to see why shooting illegal drugs like heroin with someone else's needle is potentially dangerous. But the fact is, in some parts of the world, even legal intravenous drug use has resulted in the spread of hepatitis C. In many countries where medical facilities lack proper funding, or where sterile needles are not available, sick patients receive drug injections intended to treat their illnesses but that wind up delivering the hepatitis C virus.

The World Health Organization (WHO) estimates that between 2.3 and 4.7 million people are infected with hepatitis C each year as a direct result of using contaminated syringes and needles.

In Egypt, for example, researchers found that almost two decades ago a huge number of people seeking treatment for a parasitic disease called schistosomiasis were infected with the hepatitis C virus when they were injected with improperly sterilized needles. These people in turn spread the disease to others in the country, and over the years more and more people have become infected. Today almost 13 percent of the Egyptian population is infected with HCV. Many people have died as a result, and many others are dying as their livers slowly break down.

The situation in Egypt is just one example of how dirty needles can lead to a hepatitis C epidemic. In an attempt to prevent similar disease outbreaks in the future, WHO and several other organizations have joined together to create what they call the Safe Injection Global Network, or SIGN.

SIGN has several major goals. Their first goal is to get health-care workers in countries worldwide to rely less on injections for treating disease and more on other methods, like pills that can be taken by mouth. Another goal is to teach those health-care workers who do have to administer injections how to do so safely. SIGN stresses the need for sterile syringes and needles, and recommends that needles and other dangerous medical wastes be disposed of and destroyed immediately after use. Only then can the

Contracting the Hepatitis C Virus

spread of hepatitis C by injection be brought to an end.

"Although most injections given in the world follow safe clinical practices, poor injection practices continue to transmit viral hepatitis and other infections on a large scale in many countries. Appropriate measures can and must be taken to avoid this route of transmission of disease," says Dr. Yvan Hutin, Blood Safety and Clinical Technology Department, World Health Organization.

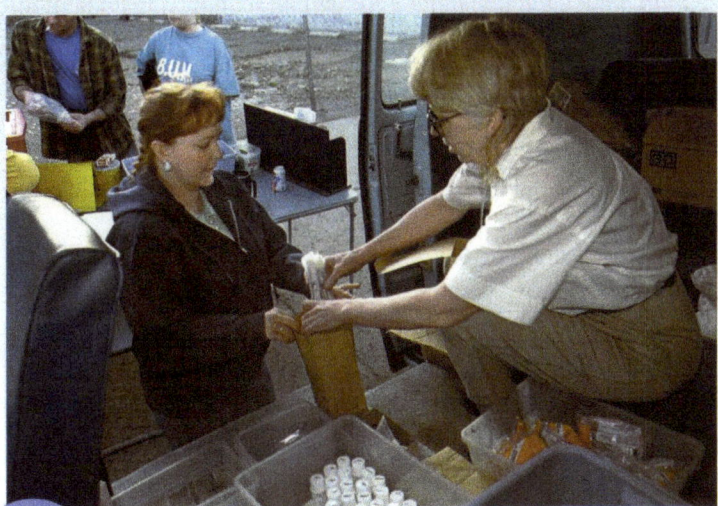

Needle exchange programs provide clean needles to drug addicts, helping prevent the spread of hepatitis C.

It doesn't matter who the partners are or what their sexual preferences happen to be. Blood-to-blood transmission may happen between partners of the same sex. All it takes is the mingling of blood from an infected person with blood from the other. Of course, the more you have unprotected sex, the greater your risk. And if you choose to have unprotected sex with more than one partner, the risk multiplies.

Blood Transfusions

Sometimes very sick people require a medical process known as a blood transfusion. In a blood transfusion, a healthy person donates some of his or her blood to a sick patient. Doctors use special techniques to move the donor's blood into the patient's body. This donation doesn't hurt the donor at all, and it often saves the life of the recipient.

Unfortunately, prior to 1990, scientists didn't know enough about hepatitis C to effectively screen for the disease in blood donors. Because of this, many people who received blood transfusions in the years before 1990 wound up contracting the virus when they were unknowingly given blood from infected donors. Some of these people still don't know that they have hepatitis C.

Today doctors have very sophisticated tests that allow them to check donors' blood for the hepatitis C antibody. Antibodies are special fighter molecules the body creates in an attempt to hunt down and destroy specific viruses.

Contracting the Hepatitis C Virus

If the hepatitis C antibody is present in a person's blood, it's a good indicator that the virus is there as well.

This screening technology is now routine—at least in countries such as the United States. In fact, your chances of getting hepatitis C from blood transfusions today are less than one in a million. Considering the fact that transfusions regularly save lives, these are very good odds.

Birth to an Infected Mother

Fortunately, for reasons not very well known, it's uncommon for hepatitis C to be spread from an infected mother to her unborn infant. Less than 5 percent of infants born to hepatitis C–infected women become infected as a result. When babies do contract hepatitis C from their mothers, they usually have very few symptoms of the disease. Sometimes they have no symptoms at all. Many healthy infants have traces of their mothers' hepatitis C antibodies in their blood, but these antibodies normally disappear after about a year.

Other Exposures

Health-care workers—like nurses, emergency medical technicians, and doctors—must take special precautions every time they treat a patient. These precautions are necessary because coming in contact with a patient's blood, whether through needle pricks, surgical procedures, or other work-related contact, could result in exposure to hepatitis C and other diseases.

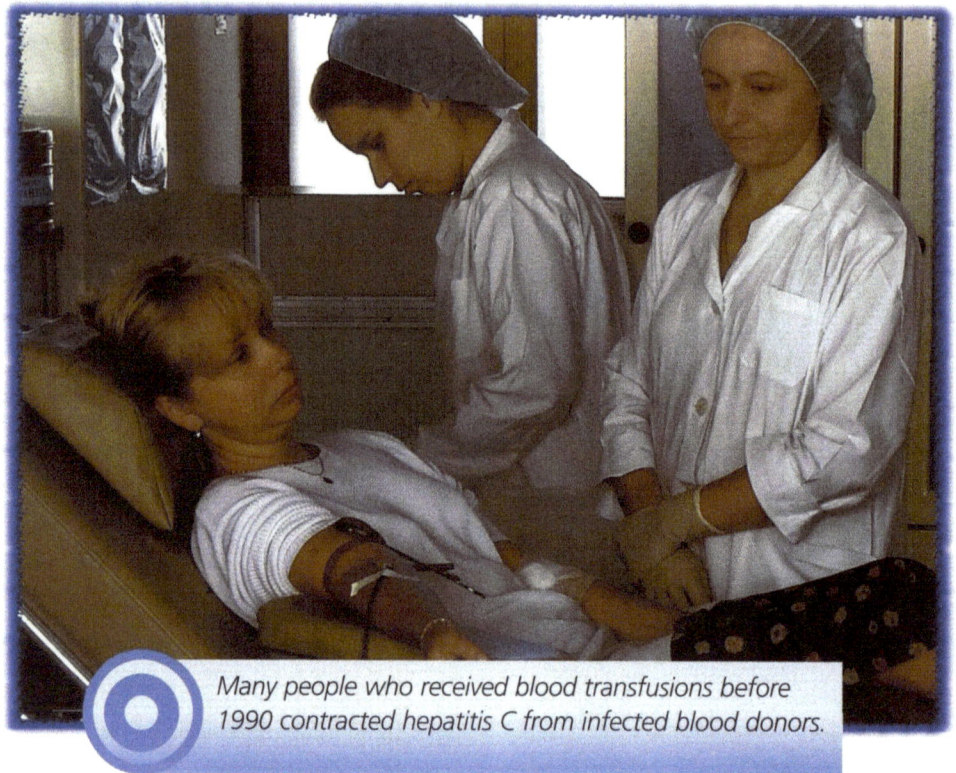

Many people who received blood transfusions before 1990 contracted hepatitis C from infected blood donors.

One thing health-care professionals do to protect themselves is wear protective clothing designed to shield them from blood. They wear latex gloves, protective gowns and eyewear, and surgical masks. They dispose of dangerous needles in specially designed medical-waste bins, and they always take great care any time they draw blood or help a bleeding patient.

The sharing of other potential blood carriers, like toothbrushes or razors, can also result in transmission of hepatitis C. Special care should be taken to ensure that personal items that could come into contact with blood are not shared.

Contracting the Hepatitis C Virus

Unknown Exposures

An estimated 10 percent of people who are infected with hepatitis C have no idea how they got the disease. Doctors say these people have "community-acquired" hepatitis C. This means they somehow acquired the disease through their community, the people with whom they've come in contact over the years, whether directly or through medical procedures involving the transfer of blood. While such people may not know their disease's cause, in all cases one thing is certain: Blood-to-blood contact with an infected person must have taken place at some point, whether through sexual intercourse, cuts, medical injections, operations, or other means.

Keeping Free of Hepatitis-C

It's easy to avoid getting hepatitis C. You just have to be responsible for your actions and be careful and thoughtful when you're doing certain things.

For one, don't use needles to take drugs. Drugs are dangerous enough without the threat of disease from an infected needle. But if you do use needles, use a new needle every time. Sharing needles is out of the question. No matter how well you think you might know someone, they could have hepatitis C or another blood-borne illness. Sharing needles is not worth the risk.

Hepatitis C

You Can't Get Hepatitis C By . . .

With millions of people infected with the hepatitis C virus worldwide, you might think you could get hepatitis C really easily. But that's not the case. Here are some of the ways you definitely cannot get hepatitis C:

- You can't get hepatitis C by shaking hands with an infected person.
- You can't get hepatitis C through a hug.
- You can't get hepatitis C from a cough or a sneeze.
- You can't get hepatitis C by sitting next to or hanging around an infected person.
- You can't get hepatitus C by receiving an injection with a sterile needle from your doctor.
- You have to make direct contact with an infected person's blood to get hepatitis C, and even then, you may not get it.

Contracting the Hepatitis C Virus

Tattoo? You Might Want to Wait

You probably know someone with a tattoo. Tattoos have become very popular, and lots of people have them. For the most part getting a tattoo is a very safe process, but some studies have found a potential link between tattooing and hepatitis C infection. In tattooing, needles are inserted beneath the skin's surface. There is a slight risk that blood-borne diseases such as hepatitis C can be accidentally passed into the bloodstream when tattooing tools are not properly cleaned and sterilized.

The CDC is currently conducting a large study designed to determine whether tattooing is in fact risky. For now, however, there's no conclusive evidence that it is—when it's done properly. Of course, if you are thinking about getting tattooed, you should take a few precautions. Never go to a tattoo parlor without

Hepatitis C

> doing a little research beforehand. Check to make sure the shop sterilizes, and see if it's a professional establishment, not just some hole in the wall with a lousy reputation. If you're still not sure when you're through checking things out, maybe you should wait. After all, tattoos are permanent. Once they're on, it's a real pain to have them removed. For the latest on the CDC study, see its hepatitis C Web page at http://www.cdc.gov/ncidod/diseases/hepatitis/c.

Another thing you can do is protect yourself from other people's blood if you have to come in contact with it. For instance, if you're helping a friend who has a cut, wear protective gloves. You'll notice that nurses and doctors always wear special latex gloves when they draw or handle their patients' blood.

If you get a tattoo or a body piercing, make sure you get it from a professional who cleans his or her tools. If you have any doubt that their piercing tools are not clean and sterile, go somewhere else to get the job done.

Finally, if you're going to have sex, use a condom. Condoms not only prevent pregnancies, they also prevent swapping of other bodily fluids, like blood, during intercourse.

Chapter 3
Getting Tested for Hepatitis C

Because hepatitis C is such a "sleeper" disease, few people go to their doctors strictly for a hepatitis C test. In fact, the majority of people with hepatitis C find out they have the disease when they go to their local hospital or blood bank and try to donate blood. Blood donors are automatically screened for hepatitis C and other diseases. When the results of the screening come back positive for hepatitis C, the donor is told he or she may have the disease and is advised to see a physician.

Another way people find out they have hepatitis C is when they go in to see their doctor for a physical exam and receive a special chemistry profile. In a chemistry profile, the doctor tests the blood for numerous things. One part of the test might focus on the kidneys, while another might zero in on the liver. The results give the physician an idea how various parts of the body are functioning. If the portion of the profile showing results for liver function indicates abnormal levels of specific molecules in the blood, it tells the doctor that the patient may have hepatitis C.

The Testing Process

Doctors normally go through the hepatitis C testing process only with individuals who are suspected of having hepatitis C. These are people with symptoms of chronic liver disease, with risk factors such as intravenous drug use or having received blood transfusions before 1990, or with abnormal laboratory tests suggesting liver disease. Most patients with hepatitis C are asymptomatic (without symptoms) or have non-specific symptoms like fatigue. The doctor might ask the patient for a detailed history in order to find out more about him or her and what the person's risk factors are. Of course, if you ever believe you've been exposed to the hepatitis C virus, you should go to your doctor and request a test. That's safer than waiting for symptoms to appear.

Your doctor won't know for certain whether you have hepatitis C unless he or she conducts special blood tests. There's no way of knowing your hepatitis C status through a routine physical. The way doctors test

Getting Tested for Hepatitis C

blood for the hepatitis C virus is by drawing it and checking it for hepatitis C antibodies. If those specific antibodies are present in the bloodstream, that's an indication that the patient has been exposed to the hepatitis C virus.

Many patients who have hepatitis C don't develop antibodies for the disease for several weeks after they've been infected. Others may develop antibodies right away, but in such trace amounts that they're undetectable for months. For this reason, an antibody test immediately after you think you've been exposed may not tell you much. It might take some time before you can know for certain if you've contracted the disease.

If the antibody test comes back positive, meaning hepatitis C antibodies were detected, the doctor normally performs a second test to make sure no mistakes were made and to confirm the diagnosis.

This second test often entails checking the bloodstream for the presence of specific liver enzymes. When liver cells are damaged, enzymes can leak out and into the bloodstream. One of the enzymes released is called ALT, or alanine aminotransferase. Doctors can tell when people have hepatitis because when they test the blood they detect this enzyme. Detection of this enzyme is one of the first sure signs that a patient has hepatitis.

Once a patient has been diagnosed with hepatitis C, the doctor typically will do a liver biopsy. A liver biopsy is a test in which a tiny piece of the liver is removed and examined. By actually looking at a section of the liver up close, the doctor can get a good idea of how inflamed the liver is and check to see if there is evidence of cirrhosis.

Signs and Symptoms of Hepatitis C

Symptoms are physical changes that happen to your body that may indicate you have been infected with a disease. Most people who are infected with the hepatitis C virus show no signs or symptoms of the disease. They go on feeling healthy, often unaware that they've been infected.

Many people who do exhibit symptoms still lead fairly normal lives. These symptoms may come and go, and when they do come they're often mild, hardly even noticeable. When symptoms are noticeable, they often include characteristics of a cold or the flu. Usually these symptoms come and go, and are not terribly severe. The patient might feel nauseous and have no appetite. He or she might develop a fever or a bad headache. He or she might also feel joint pain or pain in the abdomen, a result of swelling of the liver. Most of all, an infected person will probably feel very tired, even after a good night's rest.

Getting Tested for Hepatitis C

Some patients with hepatitis C develop jaundice, a condition in which the skin, and sometimes the eyes, begin to yellow. The reason for this has to do with hepatitis's damaging effect on liver cells. Another related symptom is dark urine. Jaundice normally doesn't occur in patients until they've had the disease for a very long time—up to twenty or thirty years after the initial infection. Jaundice is a sign that the liver is beginning to fail.

What Happens Next?

The first reaction of many people upon discovering that they have hepatitis C is fear. It doesn't take much research to find out that people can die from the disease, and it's easy to think that you'll be one of those who do.

Once diagnosed with hepatitis C, a patient's personal physician generally refers him or her to a liver specialist. A doctor that specializes in liver function and disease is better able to help a person with hepatitis C than a regular physician.

One thing the liver specialist does for a new patient is explain the ins and outs of the disease. The doctor puts the facts on the table and reassures the patient that death from hepatitis C is a very unlikely scenario. He or she explains that chances are the patient will not develop any serious symptoms and will never need a liver transplant or other major surgery.

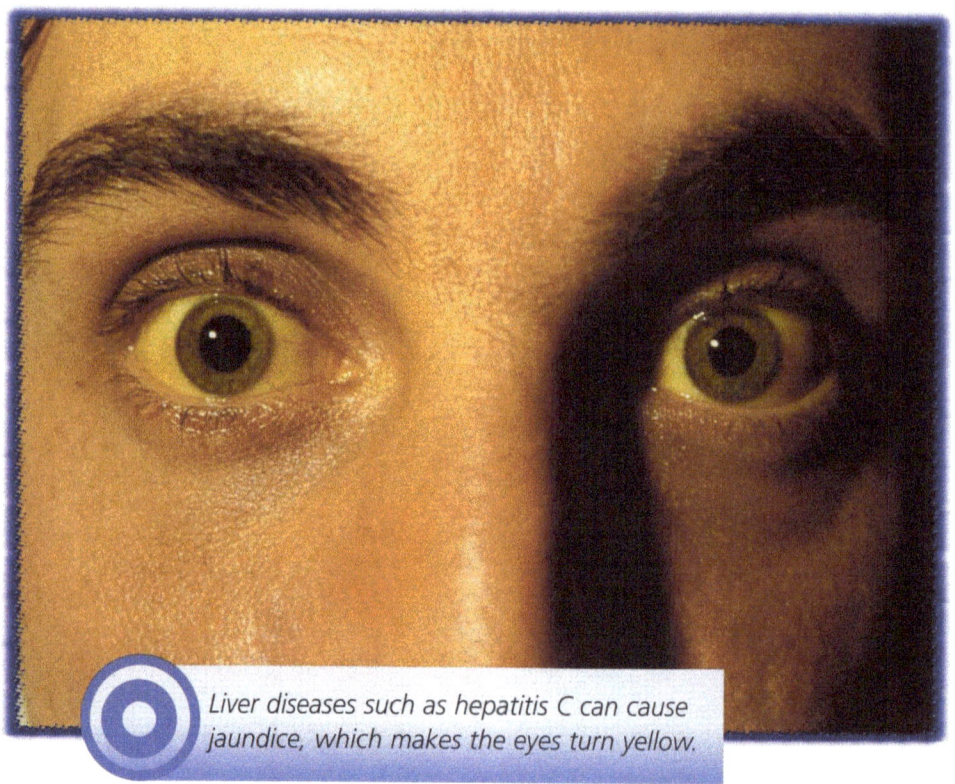

Liver diseases such as hepatitis C can cause jaundice, which makes the eyes turn yellow.

Still, the specialist is likely to ask the patient to return to the office regularly for monitoring. During the early stages of the disease, when symptoms are minimal and the patient feels fine, visits might be scheduled for every six months or so. During each visit, the doctor examines the liver and conducts tests that can tell him or her whether it's functioning at full speed.

Some tests are similar to the ones used to determine if a person has hepatitis C in the first place. They measure liver damage by measuring the amount of enzyme seeping out of the cells and into the blood.

Getting Tested for Hepatitis C

You May Have Hepatitis C If . . .

- You ever injected illegal drugs, including just once or twice many years ago.
- You had unprotected sex with someone who is HCV-positive.
- You received a blood transfusion or organ transplant before July 1990.
- You received clotting factor concentrates before 1987.
- You've ever been on long-term dialysis.
- Your mother was HCV-positive when you were born.
- You've ever been accidentally stuck by a dirty needle or other medical waste, or you've been otherwise exposed to HCV-positive blood.
- There is evidence you might have chronic liver disease.

Source: Centers for Disease Control and Prevention

Hepatitis C

Other tests measure clotting factors in the blood. Clotting factors are made by the liver to help clot blood. If clotting factors are down, it might mean the liver is not working well.

Fortunately for the patient, the liver can usually continue to function quite well even as parts of it are damaged from hepatitis C. This is because the liver is such a strong organ. Think of it as a team that has lost one or two players. The rest of the team almost always pulls together to fill the gap those players left behind. Like a good team, the liver is able to do its job even when parts of it are no longer healthy.

Over time, however, the liver may deteriorate to the point where the damage becomes too much to handle. When tests detect this, the doctor doing the testing may decide it's time to watch the patient more closely. If things look serious, he or she may even decide that treatment is necessary. For the patient, it's a tough situation. Treatment is no guarantee of a cure. It's expensive and hard on the body. People can go through months of treatment—and all the pills and shots that go along with it—and emerge in worse shape than when they began. Or, if they're lucky, the treatment might stop the disease altogether. Each individual must decide whether treatment is the right personal choice.

Chapter 4
Living with Hepatitis C

Life with hepatitis C is often no different than life without it. A diagnosis of hepatitis C from a doctor is by no means the end of the world. While hepatitis C generally never goes away for good, its effects tend to be so mild that those who have it hardly notice a difference in the way they feel. People can live for forty years with the disease and never become seriously ill.

Still, hepatitis C's effect on the body varies from person to person. And while some people never develop any complications, others can become seriously ill. Some of those who become ill develop cirrhosis of the liver. And one out of every five of those who develop cirrhosis also develops end-stage liver disease, where the liver is completely destroyed and a transplant is required. In fact, cirrhosis caused by hepatitis C is the leading reason for liver transplants in the United States. People with cirrhosis from hepatitis C are also at increased risk for developing liver cancer.

It's hard for doctors to predict who will stay healthy and who will eventually develop cirrhosis or cancer. One thing they do know is that some simple changes in lifestyle are often all it takes to keep the disease under control.

Doctor Visits

One fact of life for people with hepatitis C is regular trips to the doctor. Of course, such visits aren't always possible, especially for poor patients or those without health insurance. Hepatitis C patients who can afford to see a knowledgeable doctor, however, generally find this is the best way to keep tabs on the disease. A good doctor who knows about liver disease, especially a gastroenterologist or a hepatologist, can run regular tests and make sure the liver is fully operational. The doctor can also keep the patient updated on new treatments and new developments in research that may prove helpful down the road.

Many people go to medical doctors and receive special drugs and treatments to help them cope with the disease. But some people prefer alternative

Living with Hepatitis C

approaches to combating hepatitis C. Such alternative approaches are often referred to as "natural therapies." They deal with each individual and his or her unique experience with hepatitis C. They look at the entire body and everything that is happening to it. It's a holistic approach to health care in that it treats the body as a whole, not as a collection of parts. Natural therapies might involve things like exercises designed to condition the entire body, changes in diet, and herbal medications.

Treatment

People with chronic hepatitis C and signs of liver failure often begin a treatment routine. Treatments can vary, but they generally involve the administration of drugs by a liver specialist.

All hepatitis C drugs go through an extensive testing process to ensure they're safe for human use. First they are tested on animals, and later they are used in clinical trials on people. In clinical trials, numerous volunteers take the drug, and doctors examine them to see if the drug was effective and what side effects it caused. Following clinical trials, drugs are submitted to the government for approval. If the government agrees that the drug is safe and proven to be useful, it approves it. At that point, doctors may prescribe the drug to those in need.

The goal of treatment is to eliminate the virus from the blood. Sometimes treatment results in a "sustained response." This means that the hepatitis C virus cannot be detected in the blood six months after completion of the treatment. Most people who make it six months with no more hepatitis C detectable in their blood are essentially cured of the disease.

Those patients who do not get a sustained response aren't necessarily out of luck. Often treatment can at least slow down the damage being caused to the liver.

Current treatments for hepatitis C involve preparations of drugs called interferons. Patients take the interferons by injecting the proper dose several times per week for anywhere from six months to two years. Often they supplement the interferons with another drug called ribavirin. One benefit of interferon drugs is that the shots can be self-administered.

Unfortunately, many people experience side effects when they take interferons, including flu-like symptoms, depression, and rashes. Some people can't handle the side effects and have to stop treatment. And most patients never achieve a sustained response.

Staying Healthy

Whether they're undergoing treatment or not, hepatitis C patients all have one thing in common: a need for a healthy lifestyle. Because hepatitis C can have serious health consequences, especially for the liver, once

Exercise is an essential part of a healthy lifestyle, and can help hepatitis C sufferers keep their livers functioning.

people are diagnosed with the disease they have to take special care to treat their bodies right. One of the most important aspects of a healthy lifestyle is a good diet. By eating the right foods, it's possible to reduce the work the liver has to do in processing nutrients. This allows it to focus its energy on other functions, including the repair of damaged cells. The less stress on the liver, the better.

There are many foods people can eat without harming their livers. On the other hand, there are some foods that should be avoided. Doctors generally recommend that hepatitis C patients (as well as anyone interested in living a healthier life) eat plenty of fresh, whole foods.

Hepatitis C

Whole foods are foods that have not been processed. They're rich in vitamins and minerals and things the body needs to function. Fresh fruits, vegetables, and grains are whole foods that are good for the body.

Processed foods, canned foods, and just about anything that comes ready-to-serve in a package is likely to be bad for the liver. These foods are often high in fat, sugar, and chemical additives. Because everything you eat must be processed by the liver, these extra ingredients make the liver work overtime. To improve their diets, many hepatitis C patients decide to eat only organically grown whole foods. Organic food is free of the pesticides, herbicides, and other chemicals that are commonly used on conventionally grown foods.

Another thing doctors tell their patients is to cut back on red meat. Some recommend vegetarian diets, while others suggest eating things like chicken and fish instead of steak. Red meat can be difficult to digest and can put an extra burden on the liver.

The Protection of Others

Hepatitis C patients have the responsibility of preventing their infection from spreading to other people. For this reason, they have to take great care any time they bleed. Open cuts or wounds must be covered. Personal items that could potentially cause bleeding, like razors, toothbrushes, and nail clippers, should never be shared.

Alcohol and Other Drugs

The number-one drug to avoid if you have hepatitis C is alcohol. Alcohol is terrible for the liver. In fact, many long-time alcoholics, even those without hepatitis C, develop cirrhosis of the liver just from drinking alcohol.

Hepatitis C patients can drastically improve their odds of maintaining a healthy liver if they abstain from drinking alcohol. If they choose to drink, the disease might progress far faster than it would on its own.

Caffeine is another chemical particularly harmful to those with hepatitis C. Coffee, tea, chocolate, and other foods and beverages containing caffeine should all be avoided. Again, the reason is that caffeine places stress on the liver.

Finally, illegal drugs, and even many prescription and over-the-counter drugs, including tobacco, also present challenges to the liver. Even a healthy liver has trouble dealing with the chemicals in drugs. A liver ravaged by hepatitis C has no chance. Most hepatitis C patients do away with drugs and alcohol altogether.

Hepatitis C

When it comes to sexual intercourse, hepatitis C patients should always use condoms. They should also tell their partners they have the hepatitis C virus before they have sex. That way the partner can make an informed decision about whether he or she is willing to risk exposure to the virus, no matter how remote the chance.

Sometimes hepatitis C patients are more infectious at certain times than at others. This is because viral levels in the blood can vary. Levels may rise when certain medications are taken. People with the disease have to be aware when they're most infectious. That way they can take extra care to avoid spreading the disease to those with whom they come in contact.

In just about every other regard, hepatitis C patients can go on living life as usual. In fact, there's a good chance you've seen people with hepatitis C in all kinds of places, doing things like shopping, dining out, and playing sports just like everyone else. Unless they came up and told you, you'd never know they had the disease.

Chapter 5
The Future of Hepatitis C

Considering how recently the hepatitis C virus was discovered, doctors and scientists have made an incredible amount of progress in their fight against the disease. Each year new discoveries are made. Sometimes new drugs to combat the disease are created. Slowly but surely, the disease is being beaten. Those who contract hepatitis today stand a good chance of seeing a cure for the disease discovered in their lifetime.

For now, however, there is much work to be done. Scientists are putting all their energy into finding a vaccine for the disease, inventing cheaper, more effective drugs, and developing promising new technologies that may make liver transplants a thing of the past. Others are focusing their labors on education, feeling that the more the public knows about the disease, the less likely they are to catch it.

Hepatitis C

Vaccines

There are two major kinds of potential vaccines for hepatitis C. The first is a preventative vaccine. A preventative vaccine would be given to a person before he or she contracts the disease. Current preventative vaccines include the standard shots almost everyone in the United States receives for measles, mumps, and rubella. A preventative vaccine for hepatitis C would prevent the virus from ever taking hold of one's liver cells in the first place.

Unfortunately, most scientists doubt there's any chance of developing a preventative vaccine for hepatitis C anytime in the near future. The problem lies in the very nature of the disease. Hepatitis C has many different variations, even within one person. The disease is constantly mutating and modifying, changing form all the time. The only way a preventative vaccine would be effective against a disease like hepatitis C would be if scientists could somehow get it to stop the growth of these different mutations. For now, the technology to invent such a vaccine doesn't exist. Somewhere down the road, however, that's likely to change.

The second kind of potential vaccine for hepatitis C is called a therapeutic vaccine. Unlike preventative vaccines, therapeutic vaccines would go to work after a

The Future of Hepatitis C

person has contracted the hepatitis C virus. They would kick the immune system into overdrive, enhancing its ability to fight off the virus. Scientists are working hard to invent effective therapeutic vaccines for hepatitis C. For now, however, they haven't had any luck. Still, many hepatitis experts believe the creation of this type of vaccine is not far away.

Other Drugs and Medications

The standard interferon treatments of today are not ideal for many people. The drug has many harmful side effects, and it is not effective for many patients. For this reason, some hepatitis C experts are focusing their efforts on the hunt for better hepatitis C–fighting drugs. Their goal is to develop safer, better, cheaper medications that can reduce or eliminate the effects of the disease on the body.

One recent development is the creation of a modified interferon drug that lasts longer than the regular interferon. Because it lasts longer, it requires fewer injections. With fewer injections, patients are more likely to stick to their medication routines (imagine having to inject a drug three times a week, then imagine how relieved you would be if suddenly you had to do so only once per week). Another advantage of this drug is that it works better than regular interferon.

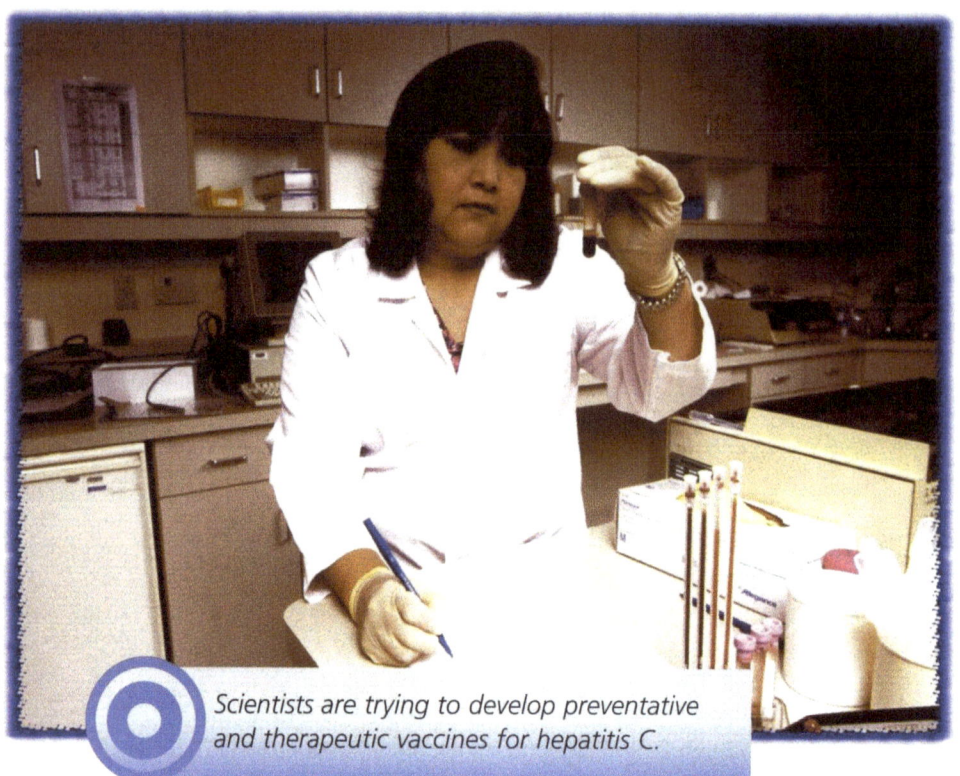
Scientists are trying to develop preventative and therapeutic vaccines for hepatitis C.

More people emerge from treatment with a sustained response, meaning the levels of the hepatitis C virus in their bodies remain reduced a long time after treatment is completed. Unfortunately, this new treatment does create bad side effects for many of its users. And therein lies the goal for the future. If scientists can somehow reduce the drug's side effects, it will be a complete success.

Another promising development in drugs for hepatitis C is combination therapy. In combination therapy, the patient takes two or more different drugs at the same time. The drugs are designed to act together and

The Future of Hepatitis C

team up on the virus. Often this combination can deliver the knockout punch that sends the virus on its way. Combination therapy is already standard treatment for many people with hepatitis C, but scientists are constantly looking for new combinations of drugs that might be more effective than the current ones.

Still other scientists are working to create drugs that can prevent fibrosis and cirrhosis. They hope to invent specific drugs that can reverse these conditions, allowing the liver to heal and nurse itself back to health. One way experts hope to make progress in this regard is by learning more about fibrosis and cirrhosis and exactly why these conditions occur. One thing they're uncertain of right now, for example, is why some people develop fibrosis or cirrhosis while others do not.

Finally, as far as hepatitis C drugs are concerned, scientists are studying ways to create effective "inhibitors," drugs that would prevent the hepatitis C virus from replicating. The drugs would stop HCV enzymes, which are essential to replication, in their tracks. They also might employ enzymes of their own that could break down the very RNA molecules that harbor the virus. At present these inhibitor drugs are merely in the experimental phase and have yet to be tested on people. Soon, however, as tests on animals bring more convincing results, that will change.

A Potential Cure?

In early 2001 the U.S. Food and Drug Administration approved a modified interferon drug called pegylated interferon for the treatment of hepatitis C. People with the disease, and especially their doctors, were very excited. Finally there was an alternative to the standard treatment for hepatitis C, a combination of regular interferon and a drug called ribavirin.

This modified drug had distinct advantages over the old ones. For one, patients would be required to take it (via injection) just once each week because it lasted longer in the blood. The old combination required three weekly injections. Also, this new drug, especially when, like its predecessor, combined with ribavirin, was far more effective at kicking the virus out of the body. Finally, it caused fewer serious side effects—something everyone was happy about.

The Future of Hepatitis C

> In a January 2001 interview with the *Boston Herald* newspaper, Dr. Nezam Afdal, a liver specialist and one of the experts who tested pegylated interferon's performance during its development, said the drug could be exactly the thing hepatitis C sufferers have been looking for. He also gave a hint at just how promising this drug could prove to be. "We're talking about clearing the virus from the bloodstream," Afdal said. "The liver returns back to normal. With any other viral infection, AIDS or herpes, for example, all we can do is control the virus. . . . But we're able to cure hepatitis C. That's a huge step."

Stem Cells

Stem cells are cells found in human bone marrow that have yet to develop any specific role in the functioning of the body. They're unclaimed, so to speak, ready to go to work wherever they are needed. They have the potential to develop into almost any part of the human body.

Many scientists believe that stem cells hold a world of promise for people with livers that have been completely destroyed by hepatitis C and cirrhosis. They think they'll be able to take these stem cells out of bone marrow, modify them in the laboratory, and get them to grow into healthy liver cells. If this does prove possible, it could mean an end to liver transplants. Rather than having to undergo painful, expensive, and dangerous liver transplants that may not work, patients could instead use new liver cells grown from stem cells to replace those they've lost to hepatitis C.

Again, this potential development in liver repair may happen in the future. The technology necessary to successfully create new liver cells from stem cells in the laboratory has not yet been proven, and for various political reasons, stem cell research has been bogged down with legal problems.

Testing

Another potential development in the field of hepatitis C research and treatment involves the need for more sensitive and less expensive ways to measure levels of the virus in the body. If doctors can provide their patients with a cheap and reliable means of testing for the virus, more people may opt for a hepatitis C test in the first place. And if people know they have the virus, they can take extra precautions to avoid spreading it to others.

The Future of Hepatitis C

More sensitive testing would also mean better monitoring of patients who already have the disease. Doctors would know exactly what condition the liver is in at all times and would be able to recommend specific types of therapy based on that condition. Today many people with hepatitis C don't even register on the radar screen when it comes to detecting amounts of the virus in their blood. More sensitive technologies would change this and give doctors and patients more control over the disease.

Education

The final and perhaps most important component of the future battle against hepatitis C rests in education. The better people understand the disease, the more they can do to prevent themselves from contracting it.

Toward this end, some health experts are working to create needle exchange programs in parts of the world where injection drug use is common. They want to teach drug users the dangers of sharing needles and convince them that if they have to shoot up, they must do so with clean needles.

Other education programs are designed to teach health professionals things they can do to reduce their risk of getting the disease. These programs explain the importance of using latex gloves, masks, and other protective devices around bleeding patients.

Sex education, too, has the potential to prevent the spread of hepatitis C. If people are shown the risks of unprotected sex, they may decide to use condoms. That step alone could prevent thousands of people from contracting the disease. It could also save countless lives.

Another goal of education must be prevention of the disease in parts of the world where sterilization of medical equipment is not always a sure thing. If developing countries can improve their health facilities to the point where hepatitis C is routinely screened for and needles and syringes are regularly sterilized or properly disposed of, the worldwide spread of hepatitis C will quickly decrease.

Considering how many people around the world are infected with the disease—nearly 170 million at last count—this part of the current and future battle against hepatitis C is by far the most important. Hepatitis C, the silent epidemic, is also a global epidemic. To defeat hepatitis C, people around the world will have to work together.

Glossary

acute Lasting a short time.

antibodies Special fighter molecules the body produces in response to the presence of a virus.

asymptomatic Without signs or symptoms of a disease.

chronic Lasting a long time.

cirrhosis A condition of the liver, often caused by hepatitis C, in which dead and damaged cells are replaced by tough, fibrous tissue.

disease A change in the normal structure or function of any part of the body characterized by specific symptoms or signs.

epidemic A disease that affects a large number of people.

Hepatitis C

fibrosis Tissue scarring of the liver.

holistic Pertaining to the body as a whole, rather than a series of parts.

infection The invasion of a host (a human being, for example) by a microorganism. Infections may eventually lead to disease.

inhibitors Drugs that prevent the hepatitis C virus from replicating.

intravenous Entering the body by way of a vein.

jaundice Yellowish coloring of the skin and body fluids caused by secretions from the liver.

symptom A physical sign that indicates the presence of disease.

transfusion The transfer of blood from one person to another person in need of blood.

transmission The spread of a disease from one person to another.

vaccine A preparation of living or dead microorganisms that is administered to artificially increase immunity to a particular disease.

virus A microorganism or molecule that causes disease.

Where to Go for Help

In the United States

American Liver Foundation
75 Maiden Lane, Suite 603
New York, NY 10038
(800) 465-4837
e-mail: webmail@liverfoundation.org
Web site: http://www.liverfoundation.org

The Centers for Disease Control and Prevention
1600 Clifton Road
Atlanta, GA 30333
(800) 311-3435
Web site: http://www.cdc.gov

Hepatitis Foundation International
30 Sunrise Terrace
Cedar Grove, NJ 07009-1423
(800) 891-0707
e-mail: mail@hepfi.org
Web site: http://www.hepfi.org

National Institute of Allergy and Infectious Diseases
Division of Microbiology and Infectious Diseases
National Institutes of Health (NIH)
Building 31, Room 7A-50
31 Center Drive MSC 2520
Bethesda, MD 20892-2520
(301) 496-1884
Web site: http://www.niaid.nih.gov

World Health Organization
Regional Office for the Americas
525 23rd Street NW
Washington, DC 20037
(202) 974-3000
Web site: http://www.who.org

In Canada

Canadian Liver Foundation
2235 Sheppard Avenue East, Suite 1500

Where to Go for Help

Toronto, ON M2J 5B5
(800) 563-5483
e-mail: clf@liver.ca
Web site: http://www.liver.ca

Hepatitis C Society of Canada
3050 Confederation Parkway, Unit # 301B
Mississauga, ON L5B 3Z6
(800) 652-4372
e-mail: mail@hepatitiscsociety.com
Web site: http://www.hepatitiscsociety.com

Hepatitis Information Network
3535 Trans-Canada Highway
Pointe Claire, Quebec H9R 1B4
Web site: http://www.hepnet.com

Hotlines

CDC Hepatitis Information Line
(888) 443-7232

Hepatitis C Connection
(800) 522-4372

Hepatitis Help Line
(800) 390-1202

Web Sites

Due to the changing nature of Internet links, the Rosen Publishing Group, Inc., has developed an online list of Web sites related to the subject of this book. This site is updated regularly. Please use this link to access the list:

http://www.rosenlinks.com/ntk/hepa/

For Further Reading

Dolan, Matthew. *The Hepatitis C Handbook.* Berkeley, CA: Frog, Limited, 1999.

Everson, Gregory T., and Hedy Weinberg. *Living with Hepatitis C: A Survivor's Guide.* Long Island City, NY: The Hatherleigh Company, Limited, 1999.

Turkington, Carol. *Hepatitis C: The Silent Epidemic.* Lincolnwood, IL: NTC Contemporary Publishing, 1999.

Washington, Harriet. *Living Healthy with Hepatitis C: Natural and Conventional Approaches to Recover Your Quality of Life.* New York: Dell Publishing, 2000.

Bibliography

American Liver Foundation. Retrieved August 2001. (http://www.liverfoundation.org).

The Centers for Disease Control and Prevention. Retrieved August 2001. (http://www.cdc.gov).

Hepatitis Foundation International. Retrieved August 2001. (http://www.hepfi.org).

Hep C Connection. Retrieved August 2001. (http://www.hepc-connection.org).

The National Institutes of Health. Retrieved August 2001. (http://www.nih.gov).

The World Health Organization. Retrieved August 2001. (http://www.who.int).

Index

A
alanine aminotransferase (ALT), 31
alcohol, 43
antibodies, 22–23, 31

B
birth to an infected mother, 23, 35
blood transfusions, 10, 22–23, 30, 35

C
caffeine, 43
cancer, 38
Centers for Disease Control and
    Prevention (CDC), 17, 18, 27,
    28, 35
cirrhosis, 13, 32, 37, 38, 43, 49, 52
clotting factors, 35, 36
combination therapy, 48–49

D
dialysis, 35
doctor visits/monitoring, 34,
    38–39, 53
drug approval process, 39
drugs, prescription and over-the-
    counter, 43

E
education, importance of, 45, 53–54

F
fibrosis, 13, 49

G
gastroenterologists, 38

H
health-care workers, precautions
    taken by, 23–24, 53
hepatitis A, 9, 10
hepatitis B, 9, 10
hepatitis C
    acute stage of, 15
    chronic form of, 12, 13, 15, 39
    community-acquired, 25
    discovery of, 10–11
    effect on the body, 11–13,
        37–38
    future of, 45–54
    getting tested for, 29–32, 34,
        52–53
    how it is spread, 16–25, 35
    keeping free of, 16, 25, 28
    protecting others from, 42, 44
    signs and symptoms of, 11, 15,
        30, 32–33, 34
    statistics on, 7, 10, 14, 15, 17, 18,
        19, 23, 25, 54

treatment for, 36, 39–40, 47, 48–49, 50–51
hepatologists, 38

I
infectious hepatitis, 9
interferons, 40, 47, 50
intravenous drug use/injections, 17, 19–21, 25, 26, 30, 35

J
jaundice, 33

L
liver, functions of, 12
liver biopsy, 32
liver damage/disease, 12, 13, 15, 30, 31, 34, 35, 36, 37, 38, 40
liver failure, 33, 39
liver transplants, 33, 38, 45, 52

M
modified interferon, 47, 50

N
natural therapies, 39

P
pegylated interferon, 50–51
preventative vaccine, 46

R
ribavirin, 40, 50

S
Safe Injection Global Network (SIGN), 20
sexual intercourse, 9, 18, 22, 25, 28, 35, 44, 54
stem cells, 51–52
sustained response, 40, 48

T
tattoos, potential risks of, 27–28
therapeutic vaccine, 46–47
tobacco, 43

V
vaccines, 9, 45, 46–47

W
World Health Organization (WHO), 14, 19, 20, 21

About the Author
Chris Hayhurst is a freelance writer living in northern Colorado.

Photo Credits
Cover © Richard Nowitz/Photo Researchers; p. 2 © Wallace Garrison/Index Stock; p. 7 © Cavallini James/Photo Researchers; p. 13 © Custom Medical; p. 18 © Mauricio Bustamante/The Image Works; p. 21 © AP/Wide World Photos; p. 24 © Reuters New Media Inc./Corbis; p. 34 © Custom Medical; p. 41 by Maura Burochow; p. 48 © Grantpix/Index Stock.

Series Design
Tom Forget

Layout
Tahara Hasan

www.ingramcontent.com/pod-product-compliance
Lightning Source LLC
Chambersburg PA
CBHW041114070526
44584CB00002B/163